ASYMMETRY

TRANSLATED FROM THE POLISH

BY CLARE CAVANAGH

*

*

*

FARRAR, STRAUS

AND GIROUX

*

*

*

NEW YORK

ADAM

ZAGAJEWSKI

ASYMMETRY

Farrar, Straus and Giroux
175 Varick Street, New York 10014

Printed in the United States of America
Originally published in Polish in 2014 by A5, Poland, as *Asymetria*
English translation published in the
United States by Farrar, Straus and Giroux
First American edition, 2018

Library of Congress Cataloging-in-Publication Data
Names: Zagajewski, Adam, 1945– author. | Cavanagh, Clare, translator.
Title: Asymmetry : poems / Adam Zagajewski ; translated from the Polish
  by Clare Cavanagh.
Description: First American edition. | New York : Farrar, Straus and
  Giroux, 2018.
Identifiers: LCCN 2018026338 | ISBN 9780374106478 (hardcover)
Subjects: LCSH: Zagajewski, Adam, 1945—Translations into English.
Classification: LCC PG7185.A32 A2 2018 | DDC 891.8/5173—dc23
LC record available at https://lccn.loc.gov/2018026338

Designed by Quemadura

www.fsgbooks.com
www.twitter.com/fsgbooks
www.facebook.com/fsgbooks

1 3 5 7 9 10 8 6 4 2

CONTENTS

II

III

I

NOWHERE

It was a day *nowhere* just after I got back from my father's
    funeral,
a day between two continents; lost, I walked the streets
of Hyde Park catching shreds of American voices.
I belonged nowhere, I was free,
but if this is freedom, I thought, I'd rather be
a good king's, a kindly emperor's, captive;
leaves swam against red autumn's current,
the wind yawned like a foxhound,
the cashier in a grocery store, nowhere,
couldn't place my accent and asked "Where are you from?"
but I'd forgotten, I wanted to tell her
about my father's death, then thought: I'm too old
to be an orphan; I was living
in Hyde Park, nowhere, "Where fun comes to die,"
as college students elsewhere said, a little enviously.
It was a faceless Monday, craven,
vague, a day without inspiration, nowhere, even grief
didn't take a radical shape; it strikes me
that on such days even Chopin would commit himself

at best to giving lessons
to wealthy, aristocratic pupils;
suddenly I remembered what Doctor Gottfried Benn,
the Berlin dermatologist, said about him
in one of my favorite poems:
"when Delacroix expounded his theories,
it made him nervous, he for his part
could offer no explanation of the Nocturnes," *

these lines, both ironic and tender,
always filled me with joy,
almost like Chopin's music itself.
I knew one thing: night too needed no
explanation, likewise pain, nowhere.

*From Gottfried Benn, "Chopin," tr. Michael Hofmann

POETS ARE PRESOCRATICS

Poets are Presocratics. They understand nothing.
They listen to the whispers of broad, lowland rivers.
They admire birds in flight, calm suburban gardens,
High-speed trains rushing breathlessly ahead.
The scent of fresh, hot bread drifting/wafting from a bakery
stops them in their tracks,
as if they'd just remembered something vital.
A mountain stream murmurs, a philosopher bows to the
	wild water.
Little girls play with dolls, a black cat waits impatiently.
The quiet above August fields, when the swallows fly away.
Cities too have their dreams.

Poets stroll along dirt roads. The road has no end.
Sometimes they prevail, then everything stands still
—but their reign is short-lived.
A rainbow appears, and fear vanishes.
They know nothing, they jot down isolated metaphors.
They bid the dead farewell, their lips move.

They watch as green leaves overtake old trees.
They're long silent, then they sing and sing until their
    throats burst.

SUMMER '95

It was summer on the Mediterranean, remember,
near Toulon, a dry summer, self-absorbed,
speaking some incomprehensible dialect,
so we caught only scraps of salty words,
it was summer in evening's slant light, in the pale
stains of stars, when the buzz of countless
trifling conversations had died out and only
silence waited for a sleepy bird to speak,
summer in the daily explosion of noon, when even
the cicadas fainted, that summer, when the azure water
opened, welcoming, so welcoming
that we forgot completely about amphoras lying
for thousands of years on the sea bottom, in darkness,
in solitude; it was summer, remember,
when the privet leaves, always green, laughed,
it was July, when we first befriended
that little black cat
who seemed so intelligent to us,
it was the same summer when, in Srebrenica,

men and boys were being killed;
and there were countless dry shots,
and no doubt also heat and dust,
and cicadas, mortally afraid.

MARATHON

Marathoners, just after the race, proud and exhausted,
in capes blazoned with the name *Bank of America*
congregate on Chicago's main street
like ancient heroes,
parade before Sunday strollers,
pose happily for photos, countless flashes
illuminate the air.

Then evening falls,
heroics slowly evaporate,
the good moon returns,
benign as always.
Purple clouds in the sky
can tell us nothing.
Once more the world hushes.

SUITCASE

Krakow was overcast that morning, the hills steamed.
It was raining in Munich, in valleys the Alps
lay hidden and heavy as stones.

Only in Athens did I glimpse the sun, it
turned the air, the whole air,
the whole immense flotilla of the air
to trembling gold.

As the religious writers say: I suddenly
became a new man.

I'm just a tourist in the visible world,
one of a thousand shadows
drifting through airports' vast halls—

and my green suitcase, like a faithful dog, follows me
on little wheels.

I'm just an absentminded tourist
but I love the light.

MR. WLADZIU

Mr. Wladziu was a barber (haircuts, men's and
women's, on Karmelicka Street). Short and slight.
Interested in one thing only: angling.
He liked to talk about the ways of fish,
how drowsy they become in winter, when the cold
is biting, murderous, almighty,
how you must respect their sleep. They rest
then, lie in the dense water like clocks,
like new arrivals from another planet. They're different.
Mr. Wladziu even represented Poland
once or twice in angling,
but something went wrong, I don't remember what,
too hot, or maybe rain, or low-lying clouds.
By the time he got to the doctor, it was too late.
Karmelicka Street didn't notice his departure:
the trams shriek on the curve,
the chestnuts bloom ecstatically each year.

MANDELSTAM IN THEODOSIA

Let me go; I wasn't made for jail.

—OSIP MANDELSTAM

(arrested in Theodosia in 1920)

Mandelstam was not mistaken, he wasn't made
for jail, but jails were made
for him, countless camps and prisons
waited for him patiently, freight trains
and filthy barracks, railroad switches and
gloomy waiting rooms kept waiting
till he came, secret police in leather
jackets waited for him and party
hacks with ruddy faces.
"I will not see the famous Phaedra,"
he wrote. The Black Sea didn't shed
black tears, pebbles on the shore
tumbled submissively, as the wave desired,
clouds sailed swiftly across the inattentive earth.

FULL-BLOWN EPIC

Each poem, even the briefest,
may grow into a full-blown epic,
it may even seem ready to explode,
since it conceals everywhere immense
stores of wonder and cruelty patiently
awaiting our gaze, which may release them,
unfold them, just as a highway's bow unfolds in summer—
but we don't know what will prevail, if our imagination
can keep pace with its rich reality,
and so each poem has to speak
of the world's wholeness; alas, our
minds are elsewhere, our lips are
thin and sift images
like Molière's miser.

THE EARTH

Some spoke Polish, others German,
only tears were cosmopolitan.
Wounds didn't heal, they had long memories.
Coal shone as always.

No one wanted to die, but life was harder.
Much strangeness, strangeness didn't speak.

We arrived like tourists, with suitcases—
we stayed on.

We didn't belong to that earth,
but it received us openheartedly—
it received you both.

KINGFISHER

As kingfishers catch fire . . .

—G. M. HOPKINS

I saw how the kingfisher in flight just above the sea's surface,
a flight as straight as Euclid's life, straight and violent,
exploded suddenly into every color, I saw how the world's
    wild light
seized its wings, but not to kill it, just to make certain
that this iridescent bullet safely strikes
the rocky shore, the nest that's hidden there,
a flame, so it seems, may also be
a shelter, a dwelling, in which
thoughts ignite but are not destroyed,
a prison that frees us from indifference,
a mighty oxymoron,
sometimes a poem too,
almost a sonnet.

ABOUT MY MOTHER

I could never say anything about my mother:
how she kept saying, you'll be sorry someday,
when I'm not around anymore, and how I didn't believe
in either "I'm not" or "anymore,"
how I liked watching as she read bestsellers,
always flipping to the last chapter first,
how in the kitchen, convinced it's not her
proper place, she made Sunday coffee,
or, even worse, filet of cod,
how she studied the mirror while expecting guests,
making the face that best kept her
from seeing herself as she was (I take
after her in this and other failings),
how she went on at length about things
that weren't her strong suit and how I stupidly
teased her, for example, when she
compared herself to Beethoven going deaf,
and I said, cruelly, but you know he
had talent, and how she forgave it all

and how I remember that, and how I flew from Houston
to her funeral and they showed a comedy
in flight and I wept with laughter
and grief, and how I couldn't say anything
and still can't.

GRAŻYNA

Back then Gliwice had a cinema, Grażyna,
christened in honor of another cinema—
in Lvov, on Sapieha Street—
and Coldwater Street, named in honor
of faded maps, now vanished,
still runs along the oily, black river
(runs, or maybe just walks calmly);
other efforts to change this town
into that one were also undertaken,
countless bold experiments
that never worked,
the alchemists labored late into the night,
the philosopher's stone was sought,
spirits and places were summoned up,
powers were invoked, both high and low,
but forgetting triumphed in the end,
forgetting, round as a ball,
sweet as a strawberry, final
as judgment.

WE KNOW WHAT ART IS

We know what art is, we recognize the sense of happiness
it gives, difficult at times, bitter, bittersweet,
sometimes only sweet, like Turkish pastry. We honor art,
since we'd like to know what our life is.
We live, but don't always know what that means.
So we travel, or just open a book at home.

We recall a momentary vision as we stood before a painting,
we may also remember clouds drifting through the sky.
We shiver when we hear a cellist play
Bach's suites, when we catch a piano singing.
We know what great poetry can be, a poem
written three millennia ago, or yesterday.

But we don't know why a concert sometimes
fails to move us. We don't see why
some books seem to offer us redemption
while others can't conceal their rage. We know, but then we
   forget.
We can only guess why a work of art may suddenly
close up, slam shut, like an Italian museum on strike (*sciopero*).

Why our souls also close at times, and slam shut, like
an Italian museum on strike (*sciopero*).
Why art goes mute when terrible things happen,
why we don't need it then—as if terrible things
had overwhelmed the world, filled it completely, totally, to
    the roof.
We don't know what art is.

VENICE, NOVEMBER

Venice, November, black rain, Piranesi
in San Giorgio Maggiore still dreams his
terrifying dreams, which have long since
come to pass and today seem to bore
young visitors a bit. They'd prefer
other nightmares, long for new
fears, unexpected horrors.

The black rain still falls and Venice,
bent, stooped, uncertain,
dressed in the tattered fur
of Mauritanian façades and lace,
slowly slips into winter
like a medic who keeps knocking softly,
persistently on the palace chapel door.

NORTHERN SEA

It is like what we imagine knowledge to be:
dark, salt, clear, moving, utterly free

—ELIZABETH BISHOP

But maybe we just pretended to know nothing.
Maybe that was easiest, considering the vastness of experience,
and suffering (others' suffering usually).
Maybe there was even a touch of laziness,
a hint of indifference. Maybe we thought:
we're better off being Socrates' distant epigones
than admitting that we know a thing or two.
Maybe on long walks, when the earth
and trees loomed, when we began to understand,
our daring frightened us.
Maybe our knowledge is bitter, too bitter,
like the gray cold waves of the northern sea
that has swallowed up so many ships,
but stays hungry.

PLAYING HOOKY

But the kingdom of the dead may be right here,
I thought; this was by the Vistula,
among weeds and dandelions and crushed Coca-Cola cans,
which must have suffered much,

in March, when young, reckless shoots of grass
set out trustfully along an endless road
and schoolboys playing hooky drink cheap wine
in first, chaotic ecstasy.

So I thought then, but now
I don't know how to end this poem.
There is another kingdom, after all,
to which we belong,

visible and friendly,
the vast kingdom of the living,
but we're unable to see it—

because it's in us,
because it's infinite
and elastic.

And it holds alarm clocks, which sob,
and jazz records made of vinyl,
buttons, gooseberries,
and black lilac.

RACHMANINOFF

When I listened to the Third Concerto then,
I still didn't know that experts considered it
too conservative (I hadn't realized
that art contains not only art, but also hatreds, fanatical
debates, curses worthy of religious wars),

I heard the promise of things to come,
omens of complex happiness, love, sketches
of landscapes I would later recognize,
a glimpse of purgatory, heaven, wanderings, and finally
maybe even something like forgiveness.

As I listen now to Martha Argerich play
the Third Concerto, I marvel at her mastery,
her passion, her inspiration, while the boy
I once was labors to understand
what came to pass, and what's gone. What lives.

I I

CHILDHOOD

Give me a childhood again

—JOHN BURNSIDE

Give me back my childhood,
republic of loquacious sparrows,
measureless thickets of nettles
and the timid wood owl's nightly sobs.

Our street, empty on Sunday,
the red neo-Gothic church
that didn't take kindly to mystics,
burdocks whispering in German,

and the alcoholic's confession
before the altar of a white wall,
and stones, and rain, and puddles
in which gold glistened.

Now I'm sure that I'd know
how to be a child, I'd know
how to see the frost-covered trees,
how to live holding still.

1943: WERNER HEISENBERG PAYS A VISIT TO HANS FRANK IN KRAKOW

It was a difficult visit, though elementary particles
never commented on current events.
Hans Frank, a subtle connoisseur of art, a murderer,
had been his older brother's classmate.
What they shared was a love of music.
You don't choose your brothers, or their friends.

He couldn't quite see why Frank had picked
the royal castle for his residence in Krakow.
The passersby struck him as sad,
they moved like black puppets,
above, the clouds were ominous, violet,
below, the city like a frosted mirror.

It was December, a frosted month.
The elementary particles never spoke.

He gave a lecture (just for Germans).
He couldn't understand those clouds,
that mirror; fortunately other matters soon
absorbed him: his homeland was in flames.

Those dark streets were not his homeland.
Those leafless trees, that chill, the women wrapped
in shawls and scarves—it must have been a dream.
He skipped this episode in his memoirs,
insignificant, after all. What goes unsaid
should stay unsaid. So he thought.

CONVERSATION

There, where you can see the Earth
may actually be round: a narrow path
between idyllic fields outside of town,
on the horizon, a sliver of church tower
mercilessly sliced by a distant hill,

alders above a muddy stream,
in the water Canadian thyme
(which is an invasive species)
and the porcelain shards of a plate,

I sometimes walked there with my father (my mother,
as we knew, didn't go on longer expeditions),
in the fall or spring, when trees
were momentarily content.

Only now, or so I think,
do I approach the proper tone,
only now could I talk with my parents,
but I can't hear their answers.

CHACONNE

We know, everyone knows, that he spoke with the Lord
in countless cantatas and passions, but there's also
the chaconne from the second partita for solo violin:
here, perhaps only here, Bach talks about his life,
he suddenly, unexpectedly, reveals himself,
swiftly, violently casts out joy and sorrow
(since it's all we've got), the pain of losing his wife and
    children,
the grief that time must take everything,
but also the ecstasy of hours without end
when, in some dim church's musty air,
lonely, like the pilot of a plane delivering mail
to foreign countries, he played the organ and sensed beneath
    his fingers
its pneumatic acquiescence, its rapture, its trembling,
or when he heard the choir's single, mighty voice as if
all human strife were gone for good
—after all, we dream about it too,

telling the truth about our life,
and we keep trying awkwardly,
and we'll go on trying, but where are they,
where can our cantatas be, tell me,
where is the other side.

SENIOR DANCE

Or how, before the senior dance, my mother went to the
    meeting
where we discussed the evening's "artistic program"
and how her ideas struck us
as feeble, old-fashioned,
as if she, not we, were taking the final exams
she'd already passed before the war,
with honors, as I remember,
and also the war, all signs suggest
she passed it pretty well too, and how then,
during that meeting, she embarrassed me—
whereas I couldn't admire her during the war
for different reasons, completely different,

and how that asymmetry, that strong asymmetry,
for many years, for decades,
didn't permit me to see her
in truth's sharp light,
sharp and complex,
complex and just,
just and unattainable,
unattainable and splendid.

SHELF

JERZY HORDYŃSKI (1919–1998)

He was a poet of bitterness and rapture (more bitterness).
I think he was a very good poet.
I found one of his books in the Regenstein Library:
Selected Poems. This was why he'd been chosen.
He left poems chosen by others.

His biography: a bow drawn between Lvov and Rome.
Three years in a Soviet camp, several decades
near Campo dei Fiori.

From Rome he kept going back to Krakow,
and then from Krakow back to Rome.
I didn't know him, though I once spotted
his laughing face in a crowd of writers,
and remembered it.

If you accept the minimalist definition,
he was happy—he died in his own bed.

Now he lives on a library shelf
like a hiker bivouacking in high mountains.

A faded cover hides bitterness and experience.
A faded canvas cover: a neighboring volume,
smaller scale, has left its dark
trace upon it—so much tenderness in the touch
of two unread books.

JULY

July, the blackbirds have stopped singing.
I sit on a bench by the bank of a slow river,
I hear the hate-filled quarreling of lovers,
whom I don't know and never will.

Sweaty athletes run along the avenue.
The morning sun shines indifferently
on the calm dark water
that is apathy personified.

A little boy carries a plastic bag
bearing the garish logo *Men's Health*,
souls almost never meet,
bodies do battle cloaked in darkness.

A rain frail as haiku arrives in the night.
Light bells mumble at dawn.
While we're alive.

UNDERGROUND TRAINS

There are paintings that show suffering
and a candle's small flame; there are unhappy people
who seek comfort in vain
like a mailman wading through snowstorms,

there is music growing in jungles of silence,
there are executioners, dim streets, blind windows,
days that seem like festivals of cruelty.

There are those who cry hopelessly in cramped waiting rooms,
there are underground trains, harsh accusations,
also the ordinary boredom of talking sports,

and the terror of long evenings, and the shrieks of drunks—
and occasional moments of revelation,
when chestnut flowers proudly glow

and fledgling thrushes stumble
through the grass blades, stunned
by a May garden's Heraclitean blaze.

NIGHT, SEA

At night the sea is dark, bleak,
and speaks in a hoarse whisper
Thus we recognize
its shameful secret: it shines
with reflected light
At night, it's as poor as we are,
black, orphaned;
it patiently awaits the sun's return

THAT DAY

That day, when word comes
that someone close has died, a friend, or someone
we didn't know, but admired from a distance
—the first moment, the first hours: he or she is gone,
it seems certain, inescapable, maybe even
irrefutable, we trust (reluctantly) whoever tells us,
heartbroken, over the phone, or maybe some announcer
from a careless radio, but we can't believe it,
nothing on earth could convince us,
since he still hasn't died (for us), not at all,
he (she) no longer is, but hasn't yet vanished
for good, just the opposite, he is, so it seems, at the strongest
point of his existence, he grows,
though he is no more, he still speaks,
though he's gone mute, he still prevails,
though he's lost, lost the battle—with what?
time? the body?—but no, it's not true, he has triumphed,
he's achieved completion, absolute completion,
he's so complete, so great, so splendid, he no longer fits
inside life, he shatters life's frail vessel,

he towers over the living, as if made
from a different substance, the strongest bronze,
but at the same time we begin to suspect,
we're afraid, we guess, we know,
that silence approaches
and helpless grief

SANDALS

The sandals I bought many years ago
for twenty euros
in the Greek village of Theologos
on the island of Thassos
haven't worn out at all,
they're just like new.
I must have gotten,
quite accidentally,
a hermit's, a saint's sandals.
How they must suffer,
carrying an ordinary sinner.

REHEARSAL

Or when she said: you shouldn't
care what other people do—
but after all *she* cared . . .
When she corrected my compositions.
When she quoted, almost always incorrectly,
what Joseph Conrad
once said on the nature of writing,
when she got lost in thought, but never *completely*,
when she walked down a street of our provincial
town as if it were Paris,

when she looked at me curiously,
and I wasn't sure if
she was looking at me or at some
ideal notion of a son, when she got sick,
as usual *excessively*, and then, when
she really started getting sick
and I thought that it was still
just a *rehearsal*, but it was already
the beginning of dying
(end italics).

WHITE SAILS

Eugène Delacroix watched
the steamships on the Canal La Manche,
which had slowly, systematically begun
to replace the frigates with their billowing white sails,
and he sadly noted in his diary:
everything around us falls prey to degradation,
the world's beauty vanishes for good;
new inventions turn up
ceaselessly, they may be useful,
but they're endlessly banal
(iron railroads, for example,
locomotives heavy as a hangman's hand).
He himself painted fine horses and fierce lions,
with muscles taut under their short coats,
and the uniforms of Spahis, a lot of red, which
could be blood or exotic textiles,
and light dancing on a saber's blade
—but now only the machines remained,
gray machines and oil stains
on the sand, on the rubbish (but also blood).
There's so much new reality,

and the marvelous has gotten shy,
it's hard to locate, to remember,
to record, but still the high,
white, skyscraping clouds,
proud, haughty cumuli, they sail
over France and over Germany and over Poland,
they sail over us, faithful migrating birds
hide in them, cranes and bullfinches,
swallows dwell in them, orioles, swifts
and also the iron ships of the air,
which kill or save us.
They circle overhead,
death and salvation.

RADIO STREET

While she was dying in the hospital in Gliwice,
the hospital by Radio Street, where
World War Two in some sense had begun,
I wasn't by her bed.

Unconscious, absent,
where did she wander then, no one knows.
Maybe that was the war's true end,
since wars conclude with death and proclamations,
though silence always has the last word.

When she died, spring was just beginning,
snowdrops (*Galanthus nivalis*) bloomed,
flower-scouts,
both delicate and strong.

MY FAVORITE POETS

My favorite poets
never met
They lived in different countries
and different times
surrounded by ordinariness
by good people and bad
they lived modestly
like an apple in an orchard
They loved clouds
they lifted their heads
a great armada
of light and shade
drifted over them
a film was showing
that still hasn't ended
Moments of bitterness
passed swiftly
likewise moments of joy
Sometimes they knew
what the world was

and wrote hard words
on soft paper
Sometimes they knew nothing
and were like children
on a school playground
when the first drop
of warm rain
descends

III

MOURNING FOR

A LOST FRIEND

My friend hasn't died, my friend lives
But I can't meet him, I can't see him
We can't have a chat
My friend is hiding from me
He's been seized by a deep political tide
My friend now knows the answer to every question
And can trace the source of every answer
My friend thinks that I'm
frivolous, lost, reckless,
hopelessly adrift in floods
of irresponsible epithets
in ominous thickets of ellipses
My friend knows what anchors our life
what is an urgent hyperbole and what is merely a litotes
My friend never leaves his house
at night not even in May when all
the houses sing and swallows vanish in the sky
for a long time and come back happy

carefree, renewed
My friend fell in love with the nation
but the nation is serious and never strolls even
in May it keeps watch, my friend
has no time for metaphors or *pars pro toto*
My friend is hiding from me
My friend lives

J U N G L E

But it's pure accident: a Silesian city,
slag heaps on the skyline, on the street old people
speak a language carried from the East,
then discovering music, Brubeck, Charlie Parker,
a Rachmaninoff concert and the Seventh Symphony,
discovering something different, completely different,
music strange and lovely from the start, like Greta Garbo
in a spy film, surrounded by ordinary types,
and the first poetry that spoke to me,
a bookshop display, like an auction of fine manners,
but also the fat priest in a stained cassock
and the teacher of false history with a vulture's sharp face,
school dances where the girls, so ordinary,
were suddenly transformed into enigmatic beings,
the main street (we saw it as a fragment
of a great metropolis), and suburban gardens, smelling
first of weeds and then, in autumn, of bonfires' sustaining
    smoke.
This is exactly why that strange arrangement of black
and white, green and blue—mostly black

—not ideas, not the serenity of some philosopher's study,
not an engineer's sketches, or my father's stenography,
just chaos, a chaos of stains, sounds, and scents,
a jungle, a splendid chaos that you spend
the rest of your life trying to comprehend, to organize,
in vain, since there's never enough time,
enough attention, and so it remains, slipshod, a rough draft,
covered in slanting, violet lines,
a rough draft, whose cardboard covers
curl like a bat's wings, a notebook
that fades and vanishes in the abyss
of the bottom drawer, vanishes, but is in fact
immortal.

RUTH

IN MEMORY OF RUTH BUCZYŃSKA

She survived the war in Tarnopol. In darkness and in semi-
   darkness. In fear.
She was afraid of rats and heavy boots, loud conversations,
   screams.
She died just now, in darkness, in a hospital ward's white
   quiet.
She was a Jew. Sometimes she didn't know what that meant.
It's simple and incomprehensible, like algebra.
At times she tried to work it through. The Gestapo knew
   exactly what it meant
to be a Jew. The great philosophical tradition helped,
definitions sharp as knives, direct as a Buddhist arrow.
She was beautiful. She should have died then, like the other
   men and women,
vanished without a trace, gone without elegies, like so many
   others,
like the air, but she lived a long time, in daylight, in the sun,
in the daily air, the oxygen of ordinary Krakow.

Sometimes she couldn't understand what it meant to be
    beautiful.
The mirror kept still, it didn't know the philosophical
    definitions.
She didn't forget those other times, but hardly ever
mentioned them. Once only she told this story:
her beloved cat wouldn't stay in the ghetto, twice
it went back to the Aryan side at night. Her cat
didn't know who Jews were, what the Aryan side meant.
It didn't know, so it shot to the other side like an arrow.
Ruth was a lawyer and defended others. Maybe that was why
    she lived so long.
Because there are so many others, and they need defending.
Prosecutors multiply like flies, but defenders are few.
She was a good person. She had a soul. We seem to know
what that means.

MANET

The worried artist smokes a cigar,
he seems dissatisfied,
nothing turns out today.

It's breakfast in the studio,
a lemon sliced as in Dutch paintings.
But look, the model, a young man

in a black frock coat, is in splendid form:
resting against a table, he looks at us
with the arrogant gaze

best suited to happy creatures
whose only purpose
is to seem, to shine, and who

are otherwise untroubled.
They know they'll live forever—
though without memory.

A TRIP FROM LVOV

TO SILESIA IN 1945

And again the rusty cars trundle slowly
the locomotive wheezes
and repeats "A" and "A" and "A"
The freight car wheels clatter
then a dreary silence falls
the train stands for a long time in the yellow grass
heavy military transports pass it by
This train does not have right of way
it's not the firstborn son
It's been switched to a side track near Krakow
far from the city, from Wawel Castle and the Market
far from the old university
and its elegant professors
It set out on my father's name day
and Mrs. Kolmer brought a fedora cake
to the station, it didn't last long
Behind us lay mass graves
and homeless suffering

Now we are homeless
and there is only this moment
and glistening spiderwebs and hawthorn bushes
I don't know what music is
I don't know the map I haven't read Leśmian
I can't begin to guess that school
with its Prussian bricks will smell
of Bismarck brown, drafting triangles and scars
or that our four-person family
will be as perfect as the finest square
but then will fall like Byzantium
and that Saint Francis will walk
past us but incognito alas
and that ideas will turn up in their Sunday best
just like Mazovian or Silesian folk dancers
in starched skirts
and high polished shoes
It's October and the golden trees
obey the wind and are afraid of hail
and rooks (rooks are so black)
and I still know nothing
I don't even know that I'll fall ill in a moment
and will be saved along the way
by Doctor Kochanowski

HIGHWAY

I was maybe twenty.
In the junkyard under the viaduct built
by Hitler I hunted for relics from that war, relics
of the iron age, bayonets and helmets of whichever
army, I didn't care, I dreamed of great discoveries—
just as Heinrich Schliemann once
sought Hector and Achilles in Asia Minor,
but I found neither bayonets
nor gold, only rust was everywhere,
rust's brown hatred; I was afraid
that it might penetrate my heart.

WAKE UP

Wake up, my soul.
I don't know where you are,
where you're hiding,
but wake up, please,
we're still together,
the road is still before us,
a bright strip of dawn
will be our star.

PUBLIC SPEAKING CONTEST

Or when she told us, for the tenth time maybe,
about the public speaking contest that, as a young
law student, she'd won, nearly won, even though
she faced serious competition, and like everyone else,
was stunned that a woman had won, nearly won,
and not a man, a future judge or lawyer;
she came out the best, nearly the best, though technically
speaking someone else took home first prize—
and that was her greatest success,
and when we listened to her story, later, much later,
ironically, a little bored, thinking: "you're still
caught up in a competition, invisible this time,
like most such occupations,
and you want us to give you the laurels
that they refused you then,"
and how I wish I could hear
her tell the story again
about the contest she nearly won,
and in which, I think, after decades
of her memory's unceasing labor,
she finally carried the day.

PENCIL

Angels no longer have time for us;
they labor now for unborn generations—
hunched over school notebooks
they write, they scribble, then correct
complex diagrams
for future happiness,
with a thick yellow pencil
clenched between their teeth—
like first-graders
under the eye of a teacher
smiling benignly.

KRZYS MICHALSKI DIED

Krzys Michalski died suddenly.
Of all the people I know, he's the only one
who might have seemed slightly immortal.
Combative, towering over others. Fantastically intelligent.
He did so many good things. When you thought of him,
the word *success* emerged from the cave where
it ordinarily vegetates. Success, true success.
Not *requiem* or other touching knickknacks.
He always seemed to fly *business class*,
and stayed only in the very best hotels.
He made friends with the pope, with presidents,
but never stopped being a philosopher, that is,
an invisible man, someone who listens closely.
Who slips occasionally into the cave of thought.
A difficult combination, impossible.
But only the impossible can be marvelous.
In a well-cut black jacket, slender,
dressed like a traveler who prepares to set out
on a great journey and doesn't want to betray anyone
wherever he's going.

BERTOLT BRECHT

IN ETERNITY

Your grave lies right in Berlin's heart,
in that elite, philosophical cemetery
where they won't bury just anyone, where

Hegel and Fichte rest like rusty anchors
(their ships sink into the abyss of textbooks).

Your bizarre errors, your worship of doctrine
lie beside you like axes and spears in Neolithic graves,
equally useful, equally necessary.

You chose East Germany, but also kept
an Austrian passport just in case.

You were a cautious revolutionary—but can an oxymoron
save the world?

You wrote a poem "To Those Born Later"—you hoped the
    future
too would yield to your persuasion. But the future has passed.

Those born later drift indifferently through the graves—like
    tourists in museums
who look mainly at the labels under paintings.

It's April, a cool and sunny day, black shadows cling
to the tombstones, as if detectives were the true immortals.

RUE ARMAND SILVESTRE

Armand Silvestre, a Parnassian, once renowned,
now a forgotten poet and *conteur*, so Wikipedia says;
a street in no way different from other arteries
planted with mannerly trees, beneath which
sparrows continuously danced the Lambeth Walk and shimmy.
Graced by a Franprix shop, a day care, a pharmacy, a barber,
a red-faced butcher, always smiling, as if
quartering meat were his greatest delight,
an elementary school and two bad restaurants.
That was our street, rather long—unfortunately,
it lacked a proper conclusion,

like certain films, and our building, an enormous structure,
too large, called Le Tripode, the tripod,
as in Delphi, but no Pythia stood over it,
no prophetic mists rose, there was no magic
(only brief moments, which didn't fade),
and we didn't know what would be, we lived in darkness
and in hope, as others live, inhabitants

of Dresden or Warsaw, who each night
take their watches from their wrists
and in their dreams are as free as swimmers
in eternity's Atlantic.

NOCTURNE

Sunday afternoons, September: my father listens
to a Chopin concerto, distracted
(music for him was often just a backdrop
for other activities, work or reading),
but after a moment, he puts the book aside, lost in thought;
I think one of the nocturnes
must have moved him deeply—he looks out the window
(he doesn't know I'm watching), his face
opens to the music, to the light,

and so he stays in my memory, focused,
motionless, so he'll remain forever,
beyond the calendar, beyond the abyss,
beyond the old age that destroyed him,
and even now, when he no longer is, he's still
here, attentive, book to one side,
leaning in his chair, serene,
he listens to Chopin, as if that nocturne
were speaking to him, explaining something.

ORANGE NOTEBOOK

That drunk in the Planty Gardens looked a little like Arthur
Schopenhauer, he was sound asleep, snoring.

Last night, new ideas, notes, music.
Morning— a wasteland.

A whole life is contained in every day. It must
squeeze through the day, like a young cat awkwardly exiting
a tree.

Le petit bleu. When I first arrived in Paris, they'd
just eliminated the pneumatic post. The pneuma of Paris
    flickered out.

Three Caesars. Above a dirty little river. Rooks.

The kingdom of the dead is beautiful.

Praxiteles' Hermes. We're helpless vis-à-vis perfection.
Countless flashes. The face of Hermes. Tourists are souls
doing penance.

One closes, another opens.

A June storm blesses the train. A pheasant lands heavily
in a wheat field, like the first helicopter.

Aphorisms, fine, but how long can you be right?

Józef Czapski frequently advised me: when you're having a
    bad day, paint
a still life.

Express train, June, a calm evening, the light retreats
peaceably. Deer beside the forest. Happiness.

Dark poems. Summer mornings, gleaming.

COUSIN HANNES

Hannes was a pastor in Zurich.
He took me once, at my request,
to Joyce's grave, and Thomas Mann's,
and laughed at me for being a necrophiliac,
a literary graveophile, and he also liked
to joke that I knew everything
from books, though I still
hadn't been anywhere, seen anything.
He thought my passion for writing
(incomprehensible) poems might
pass some day and I'd take up
ideas, as intelligent people do;
he was good-hearted, he helped distant relatives
and strangers, still his own children
viewed him quite critically.
Fridays and Saturdays he was off-limits:
he would write Sunday's homily
and volumes of theology would mount
on the wooden floor of his study
like black sphinxes in the desert.

He died suddenly, still quite young,
and left so many matters unexplained,
and they still hover over us,
day and night.

OUR NORTHERN CITIES

Our northern cities doze on the plains
Their walls, thick walls, know everything about us
They are prisons, usually quite good-natured
We walk beneath mighty ceilings
The wind mutters in the leafless branches of trees
Our homes. Our northern cities,
their heavy clocks hanging on towers
like pumpkins in autumn gardens
Our hospitals in grim edifices, our courts,
dreary post offices built of red brick
firemen in silver helmets
Our mute streets, still waiting
Northern cities are introverts
They seem mighty, indestructible
but are in fact rather shy
We're born in them and we die
We like the scorched landscapes of the south,
deep blue seas etched
with white ribbons of waves, brown rocks,
tamarisk and fig trees, smelling of sweet fruit,

but we're chained to northern cities
and can't betray them,
we're forbidden to abandon
our dark cities, their long winters,
their dirty underwear of melting snow,
shame, sorrow, exhaustion
We must speak in their name,
keep watch, call out.